RELIGION AND THE PUBLIC SCHOOLS

THE BURTON LECTURE

THE INGLIS LECTURE

1965

Religion

AND THE

Public

Schools

THE LEGAL ISSUE

Paul A. Freund

THE EDUCATIONAL
ISSUE

Robert Ulich

HARVARD UNIVERSITY PRESS

Cambridge, Massachusetts

1966

Contents

THE LEGAL ISSUE

Paul A. Freund

THE BURTON LECTURESHIP

William H. Burton, who died in April of 1964, was Director of Apprenticeship at Harvard for sixteen years, and taught for forty-six years in the fields of elementary education and teacher education. In order to stimulate interest and research in elementary education, Dr. and Mrs. Burton gave to the Harvard Graduate School of Education a fund for the maintenance of a lectureship. Each year a distinguished scholar or leader is invited to discuss problems in this field.

The Legal Issue

PAUL A. FREUND

Religious liberty was a function, like so much else in American history, of geographic spaciousness which enabled the colonists to set up their own separate theocracies in accordance with their sectarian attachments. At the time of the Federal Constitution only Rhode Island and Virginia (which had only lately disestablished Anglicanism) enjoyed full religious freedom. Six states—New Hampshire, Connecticut, New Jersey, Georgia, North and South Carolina—adhered to religious establishments, and others required attachment to Protestantism for the holding of public office.

How, then, can we explain the libertarianism of the Constitution? For even before the First Amendment was drafted by the first Congress and ratified by the states, the text of the Constitution of 1787 contained a noteworthy guarantee. Article VI provides: "The Senators and Representatives before mentioned, and the Members of the several State Legislatures, and all executive and judicial Officers, both of the United States and of the several States, shall be bound by Oath or Affirmation, to support this Constitution [note the dispensation from the requirement of an oath]; but no religious Test shall ever be required as a qualification to any Office or public Trust under the United States." The latter provision (which is the only reference to religion in the original Constitution, save for the phrase "in the Year of our Lord" in the attestation clause at the end) would have gone a long way to prevent the preferential establishment of a particular sect on a national scale. But the ratifying conventions in the states were not satisfied with this, and in response to the pressures for a more comprehensive Bill of Rights the first Congress drew up, among other guarantees, the First Amendment.

What were the conditions that impelled the framers, the members of the state ratifying conventions, and the first Congress to be sensitive to the dangers of religious intolerance and a fusion of the secular and the religious, at a time when some form of religious establishment still prevailed in most of the states? A whole series of circumstances seems to have combined to produce this spirit.

In the first place, of course, there was a fear of national power. In this view there was no inconsistency between a guarantee against establishment on a national scale and its retention on the state level. Moreover, a multiplicity of sects was developing, and as Madison regarded a multiplicity of secular interests as a safeguard against the tyranny of a majority, so a multiplicity of sects was viewed as a protection against any domination by a creedal group. The large numbers of unchurched citizens reinforced this position. Furthermore, the rise of commercial interests made toleration and mutual respect important, as the lords of trade had put it in 1750, "to the enrichment and improving of a trading nation." The Revolutionary War had brought a sobering sense of fraternity, especially as Catholic France was an invaluable ally.

But these worldly spurs were not the only influences prodding the framers. Ideological and philosophical convictions were strongly at work. The Roger Williams–William Penn tradition was not forgotten. The Quakers and Baptists were active, and, after all, the Constitutional Convention was held in the home of Quakerism. This circumstance was borne in on the members of the convention by an eloquent plea from a distinguished representative of the New England Baptists, the Reverend Isaac Backus:

It has been said by a celebrated writer in politics, that but two things were worth contending for—Religion and Liberty. For the latter we are at present nobly exerting ourselves through all this extensive continent; and surely no one whose bosom feels the patriotic glow in behalf of civil liberty, can remain torpid to the more ennobling flame of Religious Freedom.

The free exercises of private judgment, and the unalienable rights of conscience, are of too high a rank and dignity to be submitted to the decrees of councils, or the imperfect laws of fallible legislator. The merciful Father of mankind is the alone Lord of conscience. Establishments may be enabled to confer worldly distinctions and secular importance. They may make hypocrites, but cannot create Christians. They have been reared by craft or power, but liberty never flourished perfectly under their control. That liberty, virtue, and public happiness can be supported without them, this flourishing province (Pennsylvania) is a glorious testimony; and a view of it would be sufficient to invalidate all the most elaborate arguments ever adduced in support of them.

It may now be asked—What is the liberty desired? The answer is; as the kingdom of Christ is not of this world, and religion is a concern between God and the soul with which no human authority can intermeddle; consistently with the principles of Christianity, and according to the dictates of Protestantism, we claim and expect the liberty of worshipping God according to our consciences, not being obliged to support a ministry we cannot attend, while we demean ourselves as faithful subjects. These we have an undoubted right to, as men, as Christians and by charter as inhabitants of Massachusetts Bay.[1]

Finally, besides these motivations of expediency and philosophic conviction, there was the influential example of the state of Virginia, which had just enacted Jefferson's long-standing bill for religious liberty, under the leadership of James Madison. Because of their eminence in the national councils, the Virginia experience is of special significance.

In 1784 a bill was introduced to provide for the teaching of the Christian religion, with an assessment on each taxpayer, who could designate the church to which his payment would be applied; and non-Christians (this is important in appreciating the scope of Madison's opposition) would be permitted to designate some other institution of learning as the beneficiary of their payments. Despite this provision for equal treatment of all sectarians and non-sectarians, Madison presented his Memorial and

Remonstrance against Religious Assessments, which carried the day, the assessment bill was defeated, and Jefferson's bill for religious liberty was enacted: "All men shall be free to profess, and by argument to maintain, their opinion in matters of religion, and that the same shall in no wise diminish, enlarge or affect their civil liberties." [2]

Two conclusions seem to emerge from the Virginia contest: to Madison, at any rate, nonestablishment meant no aid even on a basis of equal treatment, and not simply a guarantee against preferential treatment; to Jefferson, the free exercise of religion meant freedom for believers and nonbelievers alike.

These questions—how broad is the privilege of free exercise of religion; does it apply to nonbelievers and how far does it protect conduct based on belief; and how sweeping is the nonestablishment guarantee; does it forbid all official aid to religion or only aid that prefers certain sects over others?—these questions, which are reasonably clearly answered in the Virginia experience, still haunt us today under the First and Fourteenth amendments.

The First Amendment, applicable only to the national government, provides: "Congress shall make no law respecting an establishment of religion, or prohibiting the free exercise thereof." Was it intended to be as encompassing in relation to national power as Madison's remonstrance and Jefferson's statute in relation to Virginia? The evidence on this is sketchy and inconclusive. One item in the progress of the various drafts through Congress is worth special attention: just before the appointment of the conference committee that produced the final version (a committee that included Madison from the House), the Senate refused to concur in a proposal that would have substituted for "establishment of religion" the narrower guarantee "establishment of one religious sect or society in preference to others."

If the precise meaning of the First Amendment is not crystal clear, the application of its safeguards to the states is even more elusive. State establishments continued in New England until the 1830's. In 1868 the Fourteenth Amendment was ratified, providing that no state shall deprive any person of life, liberty or property without due process of law. To what extent do these words absorb the guarantees of the First Amendment?

A few years later the so-called Blaine Amendment passed the House but failed to secure the necessary two-thirds majority in the Senate. It would have specifically protected the free exercise of religion against state action and would likewise have prohibited a state establishment of religion. The assumed necessity of a vote on this proposal suggests that in 1876 the Fourteenth Amendment was not deemed to have absorbed the First.

When the "liberty" of the Fourteenth Amendment came to be interpreted as including freedom of contract and then freedom of speech, it was inevitable that it should also include the free exercise of religion. What is not so plain is the inclusion of the nonestablishment safeguard where it is not bound up with free exercise; it is not so plain as a textual matter (is this a matter of "liberty" or "property"?), and this clause of the First

Amendment was historically addressed peculiarly to the national government as an aspect of our federal division of powers. At all events, since the school bus fare case in 1947, the Supreme Court has held the nonestablishment guarantee to be absorbed into the Fourteenth Amendment equally with the free exercise of religion.

II

Let me speak briefly about the law of free exercise of religion, the law of nonestablishment, and then the dilemmas posed by the confrontation of the two.

The right of free exercise, enshrined though it is, has had to give way to overriding social interests when these are put in jeopardy. The religious commitment of the Mormons to plural marriages had to yield to laws against polygamy. The religious tenets of Christian Scientists cannot prevail over vaccination laws. The religious duty of Jehovah's Witnesses to employ their families as distributors of theological tracts was subordinated to child-labor laws.

When the free exercise of religion has been upheld, it has often been vindicated under the more general guarantees of liberty of speech or assembly or freedom to engage in lawful callings. Religious assemblages in public parks stand on the same footing as political gatherings. Exemption from the flag salute for Jehovah's Witnesses means that a gesture of belief which is not a true reflection of one's convictions cannot be exacted by the state; this equally would be the case with beliefs that are not religious in nature. And it is a fact that the right to maintain and attend parochial schools, while it is in effect a cardinal safeguard of free exercise of religion, was recognized as well in the case of any private school.

One of the few decisions that rest squarely on free exercise was handed down by the Supreme Court in June 1963. It was held that Seventh-Day Adventists, whose religion forbids their working on Saturdays, could not be disqualified on that ground for unemployment compensation when they were unable to find work on a five-day week. The shadow of a dilemma is beginning to appear: does this special dispensation for this sect, so far from being required under the free-exercise clause, actually fall afoul of the nonestablishment clause?

I turn now to the latter clause. Here, too, the principle has been unavailing when it confronts an overriding claim of the general welfare. Bus fares for parochial-school children, while surely conferring some benefit on the schools, are valid (so the Court held by a 5 to 4 vote) when part of a general program for school transportation. The same is assuredly true of school lunches and nursing programs.

Moreover, the nonestablishment clause was unavailing to upset the Sunday-closing laws, regarded as they were as serving the secular purpose of a uniform day of rest and recreation. On the other hand, released-time programs of religious instruction in the public schools do violate the guarantee, though not if conducted off the school premises. And the guarantee is violated by a requirement that to qualify as a notary public an applicant must profess a belief in God.

What are we to make of all this? Does some all-embracing principle emerge from the welter of decisions? Some conclusions are clear. The two branches of the religion clause have independent force. The nonestablishment clause is not merely a means to assure free exercise. The free-exercise guarantee is not absolute; it must yield when it invades a paramount concern of public order. The nonestablishment guarantee is directed at public aid to the religious activities of religious groups; but since these are commonly intertwined with other activities, philanthropic and educational, some incidental aid is valid, as in the case of school bus fares or public aid to church-related hospitals.

The most puzzling questions arise when the two guarantees collide with each other. The G.I. bill is a striking example. Under the bill veterans' benefits could be used for tuition at divinity schools. Is this forbidden as an establishment of religion? Is it compelled in the name of free exercise? If the choice is put in these polarized terms, the answer seems quite plain. The benefits are paid for services rendered, and surely a government employee would have to be allowed to devote part of his wages to a church collection box. But the collision of guarantees is often more difficult to resolve in this positive way. Bus fares to parochial schools may be provided by the state, but need not be. The same is true of exemptions for sabbatarians from the Sunday closing laws. These are areas of legislative choice, without constitutional compulsion one way or the other. As Justice Holmes was fond of saying, some play must be left for the joints of the machine. A course of decisions may be principled without being doctrinaire.

I am dubious of a single, all-embracing rule for the solution of these problems that are as complex as the social interests that create them. I am skeptical of the suggestion, sometimes advanced, that the all-sufficient principle is neutrality—that the state must always legislate irrespective of religion, neither favoring nor disfavoring it. Such a rule has a deceptive simplicity about it—deceptive because it is difficult to decide on the functions which are to be compared with religion in order to arrive at a position of "neutral" treatment.

A rule of so-called neutrality might greatly extend public aid to religious bodies performing secular functions like education, though from another point of view this would be nonneutral, since it would favor the effectiveness of those sects whose tenets insist that religion must be made to permeate the classroom.

If puzzles and even apparent inconsistencies emerge, we must remember that the churches themselves have not escaped these pitfalls in their own positions. Protestant and Jewish groups that oppose public aid to parochial schools are not averse to receiving the benefit of tax exemption for their churches and synagogues. And, as the Rev. Robert F. Drinan, Dean of the Boston College Law School, asks in an exceedingly thoughtful study, *Religion, the Courts, and Public Policy*, "Can Catholics have it both ways—urging the secularization of the public schools when arguing for tax support for parochial schools and encouraging the communication of religious and theistic values when dealing with the mission of the public school?" [3]

III

Down to the middle of the nineteenth century elementary education was largely in the hands of sectarian schools. When the public school movement came to fruition, a residue was left in the form of less sectarian, but broadly Protestant, religious observances, against which Catholics were the chief objectors. Some further concession was made in certain states by granting exemptions to objectors.

The Regents' prayer in New York was an effort to enlarge pan-Protestantism and pan-Christianity to pan-religion through a kind of to-whom-it-may-concern prayer. The decisions upsetting this and the Lord's Prayer observance have raised a number of anxious questions in thoughtful minds, and to these I shall try to address myself.

First, don't the decisions actually interfere with the free exercise of religion by the majority? This way of putting the issue really begs the question, as an illustration should make clear. The free exercise of religion includes the right to worship in one's accustomed way. Does it then follow that where a majority in a school are Jews or Catholics they may bring in a rabbi or priest to conduct full-scale religious services every day, with a full panoply of ritual and insignia, giving the minority the privilege of absenting themselves? No one, I assume, would uphold such a free exercise of religion by the majority. The proper setting for such a free exercise would be a parochial school, the maintenance of which is also guaranteed under the Constitution.

But, it may be argued, at least a nonsectarian exercise should be permitted. With more than two hundred sects in the United States, over eighty of them having more than fifty thousand members each, it is not easy to envisage a strictly nonsectarian religious exercise. One man's piety is another's idolatry. Moreover, to make the secular courts the arbiter of what is permitted and what is prohibited in the name of sectarianism would compound the intrusion of the secular arm into the religious sphere. This was the point of the case a few years ago holding that the motion picture "The Miracle" could not be banned in New York under a law forbidding "sacrilegious" pictures.

When the "Miracle" case was decided by the Supreme Court, *The Pilot*, the newspaper of the Archdiocese of Boston, expressed its approval in a thoughtful editorial: "For some strange reason, the impression has got about that Catholics are uniformly unhappy about the recent ruling of the Supreme Court on the occasion of 'The Miracle' case. This simply is not so . . . The Supreme Court merely indicated its incapacity to define an essentially theological term—sacrilegious. No one should be surprised that a group of jurists exercising a civil function in a pluralistic society should refrain from such a definition." [4]

The real choice before the Court in the school cases was whether to draw the line among prayers, upholding some and rejecting others, or to draw the line between all devotional exercises on the one hand and objective studies of a literary or historical kind on the other. Considering the functions of a civil court, it is hardly surprising that the line was drawn in the latter way.

Second, isn't the minority given sufficient protection by being excused from participation? The key to this aspect of the case is the fact that the exercises took place in a classroom during the school day. The psychological constraint to conform is strong in this atmosphere, and nonconformity produces a stigma which is real and painful to a child. As Justice Frankfurter put it in the released-time case: "That a child is offered an alternative may reduce the constraint; it does not eliminate the operation of influence by the school in matters sacred to conscience and outside the school's domain. The law of imitation operates, and nonconformity is not an outstanding characteristic of children. The result is an obvious pressure upon children to attend." [5]

The same point was made by the Wisconsin Supreme Court in 1890, in a case involving the reading of the King James Bible. A group of Catholic parents objected, even though their children could have been excused. The court said this: "When a small minority of the pupils in a public school is excluded, for any cause, from a stated school exercise, particularly when such cause is apparent hostility to the Bible which a majority of the pupils have been taught to revere, from that moment the excluded pupil loses caste with his fellows, and is liable to be regarded with aversion, and subjected to reproach and insult . . . The practice in question tends to destroy the equality of the pupils which the Constitution seeks to establish and protect, and puts a portion of them to serious disadvantage in many ways with respect to the others." [6]

Why, then, it may be asked, were Jehovah's Witnesses thought to be adequately protected in their conscience simply by being granted exemption from the flag salute, without abolishing the ceremony from the schools? The answer is that the flag salute is, by general assent, regarded as a nonreligious exercise; a sect, however, which regards it as an affront to religious commands may simply be excused from compliance.

The question of excuse or exemption can be viewed on a spectrum of public regulations or practices. At one end are the clearly sectarian exercises, such as a full-scale religious service in the classroom. Exemption would hardly be thought adequate relief for the dissenters. For reasons which I have already suggested, all clearly religious exercises have now been put in this category. Next come exercises like the flag salute, which to some carry a religious connotation. Finally, at the other end of the spectrum, are such secular rules as those forbidding polygamy, rules which a certain religious sect finds in conflict with its religious duties. Here not even exemption is granted, in view of the social imperative of the civil rule. The same would be true, I have no doubt, if a sect protested that to pay taxes is sinful. In short, a solution by way of exempting the religious dissenter is not a sovereign remedy; in some circumstances it is too little, in others it may be too generous.

Third, do the recent decisions threaten other civic

practices which in some way involve religion with the state? What, for example, is the legal status of chaplains in Congress, in the armed services, or in prisons? The opinion of the Court by Justice Clark, and the concurring opinions of Justice Brennan and Justice Goldberg, are at pains to point out that the decision is addressed to religious exercises in the public schools and is not to be taken in any doctrinaire way as a barrier to every civil program that in some way involves religion.

From the standpoint of constraint on the individual, an opening prayer in Congress is surely distinguishable from the prayer exercise in the schoolroom. And chaplains in the armed services or in prisons may be a means of preserving the free exercise of religion for those whom the government has displaced from their normal places of worship. Similarly with G.I. benefits that can be used to pay tuition at a theological school; if the money can be used for dental or dancing school, there would be a question of denial of free exercise of religion to forbid its use at a divinity school. In these examples, the guarantee against establishment runs into the countervailing guarantee of free exercise. In the school prayer cases these two branches of the First Amendment point harmoniously in one direction.

IV

In many quarters the prayer decisions have left a persistent, uneasy feeling that public education has been impoverished, that it is incomplete and unfulfilled unless it includes a religious component. In dealing with this sentiment it will be helpful, indeed essential, to analyze more sharply what is meant by religion or a religious component in this context.

Three different strands of meaning are to be found in the call for religion as part of a public school education. First, a common education, it is argued, is incomplete unless it reminds the students of, and helps to maintain, the religious tradition in America. Second, without religion a common education fails in its obligation of moral instruction. Third, without religion a common education neglects a significant noncognitive element in education, the development of a sense of humility, dependence, and reverence. These three meanings or strands of meaning in the conception of religion—tradition, morality, and reverence—deserve separate consideration.

Religion is unquestionably a part of our cultural tradition, one that is reflected in a variety of sacral symbols that have permeated our public life. A number of the holidays we observe, the coins we take and spend, the public addresses we hear, the inscriptions on public buildings that we enter, all bear witness to the infusion and persistence of this tradition. While some or all of these may be offensive to the militantly irreligious, it is hard to see how they can be challenged in law so long as they are not addressed to a captive audience and do not call for a profession of commitment or rejection on the part of those who witness them. The public schools present a special case on both of the latter counts: the audience is a captive one, and the pupils would be obliged, in the case of religious exercises, to identify themselves by religious allegiance or withdrawal.

The question, then, is whether the religious tradition as part of public education can be conveyed without these objectionable features. The distinction here is between teaching religion and teaching about religion. It is an easier distinction to state, without doubt, than to practice, and for this reason, particularly in the earlier years of the curriculum, there may well be serious hesitation about embarking upon a program of instruction regarding religion. If it is undertaken, it ought to include instruction about the development of religious liberty in this country (a student remarked that in his grammar school they did not sing religious hymns, they sang the Bill of Rights), and surely the teaching should be enlarged to include religions of the world as well as of America.

The second strain, moral education, presents greater subtleties. We deal here with the intellectual component, as it were, of the religious component in moral education. The objective here is to train the students in how to think about problems of right and wrong without pinning the instruction to one or another version of religion or ordained truth. The objective should be to inculcate ways of thinking that can be built upon progressively through the school years and that will serve thereafter as an ingrained way of coping with serious moral issues. How deficient our schools are in this kind of training can be seen vividly in the columns of the daily press whenever a roving reporter puts a question of moral judgment to a random group of the citizenry. Characteristically the answers are one-dimensional and impulsive. Almost never is there a hint of the dialectical process or of the reflective mind.

In this area of moral education there is ample scope to test the hypothesis of modern educational theory that almost any idea, however sophisticated, can be presented to and understood by youngsters, provided the submission is in terms and contexts that relate to the children's range of experience.

A serious dialogue on problems of moral conduct will soon reach an essentially religious core. Utilitarian standards will carry a long way, and will frequently dissolve points of apparent disagreement, but the limits of a utilitarian calculus will be exposed in the uninhibited sequence of questions that is the mark of good teaching as it is of youthful inquiry. If the preservation of human life is a utilitarian good, why is it not clearly right to sacrifice the life of one innocent hostage to save the lives of a dozen others? Something there is—a religious admonition—that insists on the sanctity of human life in a sense beyond its unit value, that reminds us we are not meant to play God with the lives of others.

Suppose, however, that the lives of the group are all threatened by a common disaster and the sacrifice of a few—as in the tragedy of an overcrowded lifeboat at sea—will save the rest. What, the students are asked, is the fairest way to proceed? Should the virtues of democracy be invoked and a secret ballot be taken to select the victims? Shall the cultivation of excellence be pursued and the passengers be rated on a scale of merit? Shall comparative need of families for survival be the test? In the last extremity, who would feel capable of passing such judgments on the whole of another's past life and the contingencies of the future? Not to know all is to forgive all and to desist. The secular judge who must weigh a man's life or liberty is fortunately and deliberately circumscribed by concentrating on a particular offense; in his fetters he may find his liberation from the agony and absurdity of decision. What, then, in the case of the raft at sea, of a possible solution by drawing lots? If merit or need is an inappropriate criterion, we may be remitted to individual worth, in the sense of the overriding claim of an individual to be treated simply as a human being. In the one or two decided cases that have actually considered human jettison (if you look hard enough, all moral problems can be found reflected in the law reports), the court suggested that the drawing of lots might have met the demands of the agonizing ethical problem.

Consider a less melodramatic case which raises the issue of human merit and human worth "in the sight of God" in a different setting, but one readily intelligible even to a child not as omniscient as Macaulay's schoolboy. Recently I heard of a juvenile court judge who was following this practice in committing offenders: In his district there were a house of detention and a newer, homelike institution, where the inmates were allowed a large measure of freedom by day to pursue ordinary jobs in the community. In allotting offenders to the two institutions, the judge followed neither the principle of merit nor that of randomness. Instead, being of a scientific temper, he acted on experimental lines. Without regard to the blameworthiness of the individual or an a priori notion of the requirements for rehabilitating him, the judge constructed two groups as nearly matched as possible in age, family background, nature of offense, and so on, and sent the members of one group to the prison, the others to the home, in the interest of drawing conclusions over time concerning the effectiveness of the two kinds of sanction. A schoolboy, I surmise, would see ethical and religious issues here that may have eluded the judge. I am not sure how the schoolboy would decide the question of the propriety of the procedure, but I should be greatly interested in seeing it explored, and I am confident that students exposed to this sort of analysis would be better prepared as citizens to meet the ethical problems of experimentation on human beings that are beginning to loom large on the horizons of science.

The third religious component in a common education —the sense of humility and dependence—is a reminder that the feelings as well as the intellect must be engaged in the process of learning. Reverence for what is known, humility in the face of the unknown, awe before the unknowable—without these education would be a poor thing indeed, and dangerous as well if the measured pride of the scholar were to become the arrogance of the technocrat.

To the depth of the need, the recital of a brief ritual or a univocal devotional reading is a shallow response indeed, even apart from its divisiveness. What is wanted is something more pervasive, which can be freely shared, an experience which transports to the threshold of religion but does not enter its private precincts, as the shared experience of poetry may carry to the private threshold of grief or ecstasy or intuition. It is an experience that, in a favoring atmosphere, can be found in microscope or telescope or simple reading glass, an experience that may bring us to apprehend what we cannot comprehend.

A story is told of America's greatest scientist, Willard Gibbs, lecturing to a class at Yale, having just demonstrated an abstruse equation, tears streaming down his face, and the class gazing at the blackboard with the eyes of one who had just seen angels. No sacral symbols of that kind are banished from the classroom by any decisions of our courts. Nor does any decision, in my judgment, prevent a public school class from engaging in a moment of silent meditation or reverence, as the teachings of the individual spirit or inheritance may prompt.

The school prayer decisions are more important for the doors they leave open than for those they shut. The study of religious traditions, training in moral analysis, and the cultivation of sensibilities beyond the intellectual are all left open and beckoning. These aspects of education are all the more profound and urgent as we engage in crash programs for the development of technological prowess. These aims of education deserve at least a fraction of the resources and brains being expended on scientific education. Education of this kind is too important to be left to the professional educators alone. It calls for the collaboration, among others, of philosophers to clarify the objectives, psychologists to advise on techniques of learning, and lawyers to furnish materials from the quarries of moral decisions known as the law reports.

Justice Brandeis used to say, "I would not amend the Constitution; I would amend men's social and economic ideas." Today the need is not to reform the First Amendment, but to examine and reform our ideas and practices of moral education in the schools.

THE EDUCATIONAL ISSUE

Robert Ulich

THE INGLIS LECTURESHIP

To honor the memory of Alexander Inglis, 1879–1924, his friends and colleagues gave to the Graduate School of Education, Harvard University, a fund for the maintenance of a Lectureship in Secondary Education. It is the purpose of the Lectureship to perpetuate the spirit of the labors of Professor Inglis in secondary education and contribute to the solution of problems in this field.

The Educational Issue

ROBERT ULICH

The present controversy about the relation between public education and religion has been called "the great debate of the United States." Certainly, there is much room for debate, as is the case with every issue that has grown out of transrational opinions and concerning which the most rational person has to admit the limitations of human objectivity. Yet objectivity remains an ideal that is necessary even though it is beyond achievement. Give it up and one glides rapidly from the spheres of reason down into the mazes of intellectual and moral irresponsibility.

When confronted with such a situation, I have always tried to find some help by placing the subject in question in its historical context. Even though history, as we all know, is no reliable guide for action, at least it provides us with a widened perspective. Let us therefore begin with a brief historical description of religious education in our Western Judeo-Christian civilization. Although the ancient Jews did not yet possess formal schools in our sense of the word, they considered the religious education of the son to be the noblest duty of the father. Says Deuteronomy vi. 4–7:

Hear, O Israel: the Lord our God is one Lord; and you shall love the Lord your God with all your heart, and with all your soul, and with all your might. And these words which I command you this day shall be upon your heart; and you shall teach them diligently to your children, and shall talk of them when you sit in your house and when you walk by the way, and when you lie down and when you rise.

Thus whenever, in the period before and after the destruction of the Temple, the people of Israel founded formal schools, they demanded that the schools interpret the Torah and, in the more advanced stages, the Talmud. The early Christians, mostly of Jewish origin, took over the emphasis on the religious education of the young. It was first performed informally within small circles of converts, who anxiously expected the return of Christ. But when the second coming became a distant vision, the Christian communities established first catechetical schools for the initiation of adults into the doctrine and the rituals of the new religious sect. With the growing number of children born of Christian parents, schools for the young were needed, but educated Christians did not hesitate to send their sons to the old pagan universities of Athens, Antioch, and Alexandria. They hoped that these schools would help their sons not only to compete with their heathen neighbors in professional matters, but to receive the intellectual background necessary for the successful defense of the new faith during the many philosophical and religious discussions that were a part of ancient culture.

Inevitably, some of the church fathers were, so to speak, fanatical segregationists, afraid that the pure stream of Christianity might be contaminated by poisonous thought. Had they carried the day, the fusion between antiquity and Christianity, which brought about our Western civilization, would have been prevented, and the Christians would have remained an obscure sect, more obscure even than other oriental cults that, during the centuries after Christ, swept over the Roman Empire.

After the decay of ancient learning, that is, during the early centuries of the Middle Ages, the monasteries assumed the task of religious education of prospective priests and of a very small lay minority—men and women of the nobility—who wanted an elementary introduction to the religious tradition and the seven liberal arts. When, during the twelfth century, the universities appeared, they were chartered by the Church, though sometimes in competition with secular governments. Only after violent struggles did the *studia generalia* (this was the early name for universities) gain some independence from the ecclesiastical authorities. The practically minded merchants and craftsmen of the prosperous cities also met the opposition of the local clergy when they founded schools with a vocational curriculum, in which experienced laymen appeared to be better fitted to teach than monks and priests.

But even the liberalizing educational tendencies of the Renaissance did not permanently affect the dominance of religion in the schools. Rather, the ensuing conflict between the Reformation and the Counter-Reformation soon defeated the tolerant spirit of an Erasmus of Rotterdam and other humanists. In the elementary schools, children learned by heart the catechisms of the competing creeds, while the Catholic colleges, mostly conducted by the Jesuits, as well as the Protestant gymnasia and academies, conducted by princes and cities, set the Christian ideal of piety side by side or even above the humanistic Ciceronian ideal of eloquence. Students of English history will remember the majestic formulation of the ends of education in John Milton's treatise *On Education* (1644). His new academy, so he said, should prepare the young gentleman "to perform justly, skilfully, and magnanimously all the offices, both private and public, of peace and war." But the highest end of learning was, according to Milton, "to repair the ruins of our first parents by regaining to know God aright, and out of that knowledge to love Him, to imitate Him, to be like Him, as we may the nearest by possessing our souls of true virtue, which, being united to the heavenly grace of faith, makes up the highest perfection." [1]

The pioneers of modern public education, the Moravian bishop John Amos Comenius (1592–1670) and the Swiss Johann Heinrich Pestalozzi (1746–1827) were also convinced of the necessity of a Christ-centered curriculum. To be sure, Comenius' theology contained a high degree of panentheistic mysticism, and his interest in the sciences and in the unity of mankind led him far beyond the narrow religious and political regionalism of his time. And it is difficult to find harsher words against dull and uninspiring methods of religious instruction than those used by Pestalozzi. But both men rebelled against the ecclesiastical tradition, not because it was Christian, but because it was not sufficiently Christian. Its formalism and its compromises with the feudal powers prevented it, so they thought correctly, from taking seriously the spiritual and social gospel of Christ. No wonder, then, that during the post-Napoleonic era of general political reaction Pestalozzi's followers were unwelcome in the newly established teachers' seminaries, not by their colleagues, who listened eagerly, but by the authorities.

Also for Friedrich Froebel, whose epithet "Father of the Kindergarten" has concealed from posterity that he was at the same time an original thinker of high quality, a school without religion was a school without education. Nevertheless, he too became suspect to the ruling powers because of his democratic leanings and his tendency (to be found also in Ralph Waldo Emerson) to commingle a romantic form of cosmic monism with the Christian revelation.

Not even Jean Jacques Rousseau, that *enfant terrible* of modern education, was an antagonist of religious education as such. He only wished it to be postponed until the young person was sufficiently mature for a truly religious experience. And it is interesting that he chose as spokesman for his natural religion not a naturalist, but a priest from Savoy; the priest, not the layman, was still the mouthpiece of the divine. Nevertheless, the clergy of all Europe, already stung by Voltaire's *Candide* and other polemic writings by the French philosophers, attacked Rousseau violently. Only the German Friedrich Schleiermacher, the most influential theologian of the nineteenth century, shared Rousseau's view concerning the futility of religious education at an early age.

But while examining the role of religion in the education of our ancestors, we should examine not only the great authors, but also look at the actual life of the people. Up to the eighteenth century the large majority of Europeans were breathing in a religiously saturated atmosphere. The music they heard, the art they saw, the festivals they attended, were mostly religious, as they still are today in a remote Polish, Bavarian, or Italian village. Often religious instruction was combined with the singing of hymns and thus became a richly flowing source of musical life, especially in Protestant Germany. To miss the Lord's supper was just as deadly a sin among Protestants as to miss the Mass among Catholics. Sunday was a day of rest and inspiration—provided, of course, the tired farmer did not fall asleep in church.

Ideologically, state and church formed a unity, and the prince, together with the clergy, controlled his subjects' faith and piety. The king was king "by the grace of God." (Even today, to the chagrin of the orthodox atheist, some solemn acts of governments and their nations carry the stamp of old religious traditions, symbolic of the belief, however often broken, that politics, too, should be "under God.") The literature of the Catholic home was devotional, while for the Protestant the Bible was often the only book on the shelf. And we should not forget that to the Protestant the Bible was more than the word of God; it was also a book of exciting tales and stories, vividly told, especially in the Old Testament, and—most important for the intellectual development of Northern Europe and, finally, of all Christianity—it became an exercise in the art of dialectic. Its many contradictions and obscurities invited all kinds of mystical and cosmological speculations, many of them, such as the theosophical doctrines of the German shoemaker Jakob Boehme, carried on in the vein of the famous Renaissance physician and philosopher Theophrastus Paracelsus. And if we pass over from these highly intuitive and heretical excursions of the religious mind to the systematic forms of philosophical thought around 1800, then we find that the idealism of Kant, Fichte, Hegel, and Schelling was, so to speak, also the illegitimate offspring of Bible-reading Protestantism. But in contrast to the prodigal son of the parable who repentingly returned into the arms of the father, the idealists never did. Even when the romantic mood of a Hegel or a Schelling compelled them to revert again and again to the mysteries of the Christian faith (even the sceptical John Locke made extracts from the Bible for his personal use), they changed it while they interpreted it. Rightly, the clergy, Protestant and Catholic, felt the danger. Kant was called "the great destroyer," Fichte ran into conflicts with the ministry, and with all its wanderings through the history of thought, from Prussian conservatism to Marxism, Hegelianism was, and still is, the target of Christian orthodoxy.

Nevertheless, the fact remains that one of the greatest

schools of philosophy, German idealism, would not have emerged in the shape it did without Luther and the Bible. From its particular point of view, the Catholic Church proved its instinct of self-preservation when for many centuries it forbade the layman to read the Bible and used it sparingly even for the education of its clergy.

But whatever the vicissitudes of the Bible and their influence on the Christian mind—from strict literalism to philosophical speculation and finally to modern historical and philological criticism—all these events on the higher level of Christian thought affected Christian instruction in the schools but very slowly. In many places it is still as if nothing had happened since the Reformation and the Council of Trent. In the majority of the countries of Western Europe the public schools are still organized—and denominationally divided—on a traditional basis, and it is precarious for teachers to make use of the precious achievement of modernity, freedom of conscience and expression. A cloud of timidity hangs over them when they are confronted by curious adolescents with delicate religious questions.

Respecting their offspring, even liberal European parents are conservative. They do not want their children to be outsiders and feel that a young person should first be introduced into the religious heritage before he can form his own opinion and make his choice accordingly.

Furthermore, since in many European countries the impact of religious establishments on public life has been inhibitive to the organization of free religious or humanistic communities, such as the Unitarian or the Ethical

Culture movements in this country, many European parents feel that, in depriving their children of religious instruction in school, they might expose them to a spiritual void worse than the pious hypocrisy so lamentably characteristic of our present culture.

Finally, nothing has intimidated liberal parents so much as the rise and the cruelties of nationalist totalitarianism during the enlightened twentieth century. Whatever the failures of publicly established religious instruction, nothing—as so many parents believe—can be worse than the kind of nationalist absolutism that denies the validity of transcendent criteria for the conscience and action of man and mankind. But more will be said about this problem in describing the present American scene.

Now, in view of the centuries-old interpenetration between government, religion, and education, the First Amendment (1791) represents an astonishing act of legislation whose far-reaching character has never become so evident—and so confusing—as today, certainly much more confusing than the founding fathers ever anticipated. The amendment says that "Congress shall make no law respecting an establishment of religion, or prohibiting the free exercise thereof."

To be sure, the First Amendment was never intended to drive religion and prayer out of the schools. Rather, it wanted to guarantee the right of the states to regulate their religious affairs independent of federal control. And, as Professor William H. Marnell[2] has shown in his book, *The First Amendment,* the advocates of disestablishment did not act out of personal animosity against religion as such, whatever their personal opinions. They simply saw themselves confronted with the growth of rival sects, the Presbyterians against the Anglicans in the south, and the Baptists, Methodists, Unitarians, Catholics, and other denominations against the Calvinists in the north. As a matter of fact, in several places disestablishment existed before the Bill of Rights, either out of convenience, respect for religious liberty, or both.

It is also certain that our early legislators did not consciously aim at founding a "Christian nation," as so often has been said. Rather, they considered the Constitution a political document to be kept free from the strife of religionists as much as possible. Nor is it correct to assume that the people of North America of the eighteenth century were altogether church-devoted folk. In his book *From State Church to Pluralism*,[3] Franklin H. Littell, professor of church history at Chicago Theological Seminary has proved the contrary. If the statistics (which I have to take on faith) reflect reality, not more than 5 percent of the population belonged to any church in 1776. The fact that at the present the majority of American citizens are church-affiliated is largely due to later immigration and the changes in the cultural climate during the second half of the nineteenth and the twentieth centuries.

However, whether the population of the early United States was more or less religious or secular (and we all know that church membership is no clear indication), the curricula and the textbooks of the time prove that religion was taught wherever there was a formally established public school. State establishments, according to Professor Paul A. Freund, continued in New England until the 1830's. Even Horace Mann, a liberal who so valiantly fought the educational backwardness of the Boston ministers and teachers, nevertheless wanted to preserve religion in schools by reading the Bible without note and comment. Among his various utterances in this respect, one deserves our particular attention, because we may take it as a summary of his views on the teaching of religion in public schools. It is a part of his valedictory address to the people of Massachusetts, whom he had served for twelve years as commissioner of education.

That our Public Schools are not Theological Seminaries, is admitted. That they are debarred by law from inculcating the peculiar and distinctive doctrines of any one religious denomination amongst us, is claimed; and that they are also prohibited from ever teaching that what they do teach, is the whole of religion, or all that is essential to religion or to salvation, is equally certain. But our system earnestly inculcates all Christian morals; it founds its morals on the basis of religion; it welcomes the religion of the Bible; and, in receiving the Bible, it allows it to do what it is allowed to do in no other system,—*to speak for itself*. But here it stops, not because it claims to have compassed all truth; but because it disclaims to act as an umpire between hostile religious opinions.[4]

Nor did the majority of the teachers of Horace Mann's day or even later object to religious instruction. Rather, it was the intolerance of the clergy toward different interpretations of the Gospel that made it difficult and well-nigh impossible for the schools to transmit the religious heritage to their pupils without creating denominational protests. At the same time, the growing number of immigrants of different faiths, many of them not Christian, aggravated the situation, while the growth of humanism, atheism, relativistic philosophies, and new scientific theories such as Darwinism created widespread erosion of and indifference and even hostility toward the Christian tradition of this country. And nothing, I believe, besides communism, could persuade the average American citizen more that, whatever the past, he belongs to a "Christian nation"—so-called—than the belligerent attitude of Mrs. Murray of Baltimore, who forced upon the Supreme Court its decision concerning religious ceremonies in the public schools. Which brings us to the present situation.

THE PRESENT SITUATION

As is well known, legal decisions do not easily change the minds of people who believe in their own defense of a rightful cause. So it is also with the interpretation of the First Amendment by the Supreme Court mentioned above. Thus one cannot be surprised that there is now a movement to secure a constitutional amendment that would permit voluntary prayers in public schools. According to my information, nearly one hundred and fifty proposed amendments have been submitted to the House Committee on the Judiciary. There is certainly profound irony in the fact that a part of the Constitution originally designed to allow the states the necessary freedom in religious matters has now become a restriction not only upon their autonomy, but also on the religious freedom of local school boards and parents. Was it, so many people ask, logically cogent and historically wise on the part of the highest judges to go so far? Indeed, the formal logic of law is not always the logic of history, especially when the experts disagree about the first.

Naturally, teachers and school administrators are just as confused as parents by the ambiguous language of the Supreme Court. As far as my own inquiries from the east to the west of this country go, prayers are still offered in a number of schools and grace is said before lunch. The argument that, as a consequence of the pluralistic composition of the school population, some pupils might be offended or at least embarrassed by religious exercises, did convince some, but not others, who pointed at the chance given to dissidents to abstain from prayer or to leave the schoolroom. Nor were these teachers impressed by the possible uneasiness of a child who has to display his nonconformity (or, better, that of his parents) before his critical coevals. However, the school principals who attended a seminar I conducted at a western university felt no desire to become religious martyrs themselves. They just continued the custom of prayer because they hesitated to offend the majority of the parents in their community. They preferred not to be bothered.

Interestingly enough, those who unequivocally supported the Supreme Court's decision came from two opposite camps: strict secularists on the one side, and honestly religious believers on the other, the latter protesting that school prayers often degenerated into a mere formality skirting on blasphemy. On the whole, so it seemed to me, the teachers were less excited about "the great debate" than certain parent groups, to whom the prayer decision offers a welcome change for righteous indignation and for quarreling with neighbors and schools.

But let us talk about the serious opponents. They are aroused by the fear of taxation of religious institutions and by the threat of an unhistorical disruption of national customs and symbols, which today probably have a more patriotic and aesthetic appeal than a deeply felt religious one. But there are even more profound, though sometimes unconscious, reasons for the anxiety of many people. These reasons became clear to me when I read the book by the novelist Herman Wouk, *This Is My God.*[5] The author rightly believes that the Jewish people would not have survived the long years of persecution without faithful adherence to their rituals, festivals, and prayers. May then the loss of the Christian past not jeopardize the future of *this* nation, just as the desertion from the covenant would have jeopardized the survival of the Jews? Nations, as well as men, though living by bread, do not live by bread alone.

Indeed, such concerns about the conditions of deeper cultural survival cannot simply be brushed aside as superstitious. For every historian knows that rituals, religious as well as secular, help men, families, and whole communities to preserve their identity. Even a superficially understood ceremony may keep warm an ember that will burst into flame when survival is threatened. Many a German Jew who had rarely been in a synagogue became proud and spiritually supported by his awakening faith under Hitler's persecutions. The same thing happened to many Christians. And if rituals were merely a sort of decorative superstructure over a life of a body politic, why then have all revolutionary leaders of the past and the present been so eager to replace the old symbols of allegiance by new ones to which they would like to attach a strongly emotional, almost religious, appeal?

Nor is the problem of religious education solved by the remark of the late President Kennedy that the home should take care of it. How many do? And if they do, should home and school share the responsibility?

Finally, the proponents of religious education are afraid that with the banishment of prayer (a merely negative act that they consider indicative of the abandonment of religion as a whole) the public school will devote itself entirely to instructional drill devoid of deeper meaning, to sports, and to other superficial activities. Thus, as its enemies already assert, the American public school will become more and more a "godless" institution. Patriotism, symbolized by the daily salute of the flag and the oath of allegiance, will then be the only gesture that points toward transindividual values. But, as I have already suggested with regard to the European situation, all forms of national incorporation of the individual (even those under democratic auspices) need, besides the horizontal line of collectivization, the vertical line that makes man conscious of his obligation to universal human values. Hence, only that political education is good which reminds youth of the fact that no nation can decently survive unless it develops together with the sense of national self-preservation the moral urge to help the whole of mankind in its struggle for ever higher achievement. Without this transcendent urge, every institution sooner or later becomes totalitarian.

As an answer to these predicaments, more and more parents will send their children to private and denominational schools. Indeed, several articles have already appeared in public and scholarly journals predicting that the growth of nonpublic schools, enhanced by the religious issue, may sooner or later force the public schools into a minority.

I personally do not in the least deny that a comprehensive understanding of the sciences may help a person to transcend himself and the boundaries of national interest just as much as religion, and that a deep understanding of idealistic, humanistic, and existentialist philosophies can achieve the same result—certainly a better one than mere religious conventions. And the established churches have connived at and enhanced divisive and aggressive tendencies among men and nations to such an extent that one may ask how much have they really contributed to the progress of mankind. However, the modern national states have not behaved better. They have just as much, perhaps even more, reason for humility and a bad conscience than the ecclesiastical powers.

TEACHING *About* RELIGION

Several suggestions have been made for reconciling the secularity of our public schools with the demands of religiously minded parents. I shall not discuss such measures as released time and other technical devices, but I would like to touch on the various recommendations to introduce a course *about* the Bible or *about* the history of religions into the curriculum of the upper high school grades or the college. Certainly, such courses, given by competent teachers, could help to fight the widespread ignorance of religious tradition. And I, for one, would welcome them, provided they were conducted on a high level. But let us not deceive ourselves. Only then could such a course be reconciled with the present legal interpretation of the First Amendment if the instructor took pains to follow to the utmost the principles of scholarly objectivity and comprehensiveness. He would have to lift the whole religious tradition of mankind to the level of analytical, historical, and comparative discourse. For example, he would have to teach that the religion of the Hindus, just as noble a spiritual enterprise as Christianity, does not recognize a personal God. Nor does it condemn highly relativistic, agnostic, or even nihilistic religious philosophies, while both Hinduism and Buddhism, just as Greek mythology, encompass besides the heroic and tragic elements of life self-expressions of humanity which, because of their gross eroticism, modern man hesitates to include in the sphere of the holy. However, sexual desire, passion, and even the comical belong to the fullness of the regenerative (as well as to the destructive) qualities of life. Why, then, should they be excluded from religion, which aims at the full man? Even Christian monotheism and dualism have made compromises with polytheistic trends. When the medieval populace went to a passion play, it expected to watch not only the crucifixion of the Saviour, but also the lewd farces of the devils in hell—and this exactly at a time when Albert the Great of Cologne and Thomas Aquinas engaged in lofty speculations about the nature of the angels, of God, and of salvation.

In such a course the pupils would also learn that many events which so far he has thought to be uniquely Christian can also be found in other cults. Nor could an unbiased history of religion conceal the superstitions and crimes committed in the name of the sacred. Unfortunately, the record of Christianity is by no means better than that of other religions.

Thus even if the teacher of such a course *about* religion found the right balance of describing the inspirational as well as the doubtful features of man's religious tradition, he would arouse violent opposition on the part of the defenders of the faith, who, as a matter of fact, never have shown real objectivity, but simply want a course in Christianity, often with a denominational bias. And I, for one, would even understand their opposition. For the most curious youth might react to such a course in a mood of skepticism and believe those who, like Ludwig Feuerbach, Auguste Comte, and Karl Marx, interpret religion as a human invention which should be replaced by a more rational stage of human progress. There is, as we all know, a developmental phase in every intelligent young person when nothing is as attractive as negative rationality, even though it may be nothing but partiality in disguise. And let us be honest. Religion, taken seriously, means commitment, and all commitment creates a degree of partiality. Still more, can anyone concerned with religion be completely neutral? He may try, but if he tries too seriously he will become the same kind of bore as an unmusical music teacher.

Hence, a history of religion presented in a scholarly fashion belongs not in the public school, but on higher academic levels. Even there it may be objected to by anxious trustees as an offense to a sacred tradition or even as a clever form of "communist infiltration."

THE MORAL ISSUE

Thus, as a result of the preceding considerations, the question arises whether the future of the public school in the United States will be completely separated from the nation's religious heritage. The answer will be "yes" and Jefferson's famous metaphor about the wall of separation between church and state will apply to our public schools if by "religion" is meant allegiance to a particular creed. But, the answer will be "no" if the term "religion" connotes an attitude or sentiment that expresses a person's reverential feeling concerning the cosmic powers which surround him, which nourish and sustain him, and on which he depends in birth, life, and death. Under this aspect, how can any sensitive person avoid religion, and how can any good form of education remain completely aloof from it? And let us assume that, as a consequence of a radically secular education, such aloofness being achieved, would that not also be a kind of indoctrination in regard to the metaphysical aspects of humanity?

Therefore, the Supreme Court's legal decisions concerning prayer ceremonies in no way relieve the American public school of its responsibilities for the whole and wholesome development of the student's personality. And no legal decision should or can be a complete answer to the question concerning the inner relation between education and religion. Rather, after the liberation of the public school from denominational pressure, the conscientious educator should feel like a strategist who after a serious battle has moved his army into an advanced position, but knows that he will not be able to hold it unless he prepares his troops with a new spirit of initiative. Or, in order to phrase it differently, I personally regard the end of interference of political or ecclesiastical powers with religious convictions as one of the greatest, though not yet fully accomplished, achievements of the modern mind, for, among other similar events, I cannot easily forget that as late as in 1732—less than two decades before the birth of Goethe—the archbishop Firmian of Salzburg, a graduate of the Jesuit college of Rome, dared to expel more than twenty-two thousand Protestants from his realm. But I would also be afraid of an atmosphere in our schools where freedom from religious indoctrination becomes an excuse for comfortable laziness with respect to the spiritual tradition of humanity. If education fails in this realistic appraisal of the situation, the victory over sectarianism will be a Pyrrhic victory, a defeat rather than a success.

However, so many people will argue, in raising the issue of religion in our schools, we raise at the same time the issue of moral education. For schools are not merely centers of learning; they should also be moral institutions, and, so many parents will contend, true morality needs the support of religious convictions, just as the philosophical discipline of ethics, according to their opinion, requires the assumption of a metaphysical order. I have no intention of discussing this problem which is as old as systematic philosophy. However, in this context we cannot avoid the question whether the school can discharge its moral obligations unless it moors its teaching to a religious ground.

Now, we all know that nonreligious and even antireligious persons have been virtuous people and have educated their children accordingly, whereas many saints have arrived at sainthood after a rather wild youth, being, as it were, disgusted with themselves. To confess it frankly, sometimes the suspicion has crept on me that some people might be so concerned with religion because they suffer from such severe conflicts of self-alienation that they lose the courage necessary for a normal and natural life, like the most influential modern theologian, Soeren Kierkegaard. Subjectively, of course, these people are right and equally justified in defending and systematizing their inner experiences as their opponents. No doubt they have contributed decidedly to the deepening of man's self-understanding. But are they right objectively?

Furthermore, when I read about the moral conduct of certain pious folk, confessedly unable to imagine a school without prayer, against the fighting atheist Mrs. Murray (resembling the conduct of other pious whites against Negroes), then I have difficulty in discovering any positive interrelation between the public display of religion on the one hand and moral behavior on the other. Or can anyone prove that French morals have suffered since the introduction of *morale laïque* in their public schools?

Finally, modern anthropological and psychological investigations concur increasingly with the old human experience that the only sound basis of personal development is provided by the example of the parents—the right mixture of love and discipline on their parts, especially the mother's, and the natural relation of the child to his playmates—rather than by ideological factors.

Thus rather than become violently aroused about religion inside or outside the school, should a nation not be grateful if it has a public school that teaches honesty, cooperativeness, truthfulness, and the other virtues in the code of civilized societies? Why then add the religious issue to its many difficulties? And if the public school, as we hope, conveys to our youth a sound moral conscience, does it then not also provide a firm underpinning for a productive religious life? For even though religion transcends morality, what else is it but an aesthetic and vacuous sentiment unless it expresses itself also in moral action and commitment?

Nevertheless, a good number of religious people will always remain convinced that there is no first and second. Either religion and morality must be jointly interwoven by early forms of education and indoctrination, or neither one will yield the full human harvest. And about this proposition one can and will argue endlessly. Neither party will convince the other.

Must we then leave the educational scene of the United States with a feeling of unresolved and insoluble conflict? No doubt the rivalry between secularism and transcendentalism will persist with all its intellectual ferment and its dangers for the spiritual unity of this nation and of other nations too, for our whole modern culture reflects a split mentality.

However, are the defenders of the so-called "secular" public school entirely defenseless against the reproaches of the religious critic? In answering this question, I may refer here to an earlier statement where I said that whatever is the decision of the Supreme Court, it will never be able to divorce the religious from the educational spheres in our educational system. Somehow, the two will always encroach upon each other, simply because a good life refuses to squeeze the immanent and the transcendent into watertight compartments. The human soul is a whole; it cannot be bisected.

It will, then, depend on our teachers whether they want to be paid merely as "instructors" in a number of skills and knowledges and just go home at night, leaving the inner life of their charges to the chances of environment, or whether they think that their pupils, while learning the so-called subjects of the curriculum, should at the same time learn about the meaning of these subjects within the larger meaning of human existence. There is a world of difference between the gladly forgotten drillmaster and the teacher whom his pupils will later remember as a source of personal enrichment because he showed them that special areas of knowledge are not merely isolated islands, but appear to the searching mind as integral parts of a cosmos or a universe, instead of a chaos or a multiverse. If our teachers conceive of their mission in such a comprehensive way, they will educate free minds who, on the one hand, appreciate the depth of man's religious tradition, but to whom, on the other hand, the old denominational and dualistic conflicts appear secondary, if not inhibitive to, the formation of a unifying world outlook.

If a teacher who possesses such an understanding of human existence and would like to convey it also to his pupils, and is, for instance, a teacher of mathematics, he will make it clear to his pupils that mathematics is not merely a series of tricks, but the language of measure, and that it was the discovery of meaures and proportions existing in the world as we see it that made inquisitive astronomers out of the Babylonian and Mexican priests and caused Pythagoras to marvel at the relation between numerical ratios and certain regularities in the physical world. Most great mathematicians have been philosophers of a kind, sometimes very great ones, and many, if not most, of the great philosophers have been mathematicians. Music and mathematics have always been related. Johann Sebastian Bach, so I have been told, wrote mathematical formulas in the margins of his compositions. And a study of the minds of the great mathematicians who originated the scientific revolution in the seventeenth century reveals that they did not merely wish to produce new empirical data, but that they were inspired by the desire to discover the deep inner harmony in the multifarious events of the universe. Constantly, their search bordered on both the religious and the aesthetic.[6]

And if mathematics and the sciences, imaginatively taught, can help the student to see the world in a mood of philosophical curiosity, how could it be possible for a teacher of literature to conceal from his students the intimate kinship of a country's poetry and its religion, just as a teacher of history must be mentally blind who fails to explain to his students the interrelation between religion and the great landmarks of culture—between the rise of Christianity and the decay of the spiritual and social foundations of the Roman Empire, between the disintegration of medieval Christianity and the emergence of the Renaissance and the Reformation, between the corruption of the churches and the growth of liberalism during the eighteenth century, and the retardedness of Russian orthodoxy and the victory of communism in our time. No doubt such a historical perspective would create exciting discussions about the present when our national states are confronted with the emergent idea of the unity of mankind and our old religious denominations with the idea of a world religion.[7]

But will we have the teachers who can combine the sincere desire for objectivity (more we cannot demand) with the capacity of creative inspiration?

The answer will depend on the spirit of the institutions

entrusted with the professional preparation of our teachers. There is now a tendency even among schools of education to relegate the teaching of the broad cultural subjects to departments in the university at large. Indeed, that is necessary. For what, after all, does the liberal arts college exist? The first pamphlet that I published in this country, with the title *On the Reform of Educational Research*,[8] resulted more or less from my disappointment in the lack of cooperation between the schools of education and the university as a whole. If the university does not feel the obligation to widen the cultural horizon of the future teacher, the department of education will work against insurmountable odds. But I also know that mere scholarly knowledge of a subject does not make a good teacher. Necessary as it is, it is not enough. Just as important is the teacher's capacity of getting the intellectual material, accumulated in the course of centuries of specialization, out of the academic storehouses in order to render it vital and meaningful to the young learner. Only in very rare cases can this process of transformation be taught by the typical academic courses in the sciences and the humanities. It is not even their purpose. Nor can it be their purpose to relate their instruction to the functions and responsibilities which the teacher will have to discharge in his community. Our society expects from him more than the instructing of children; rather, it wants his advice concerning the guidance of the young, the resolutions of parents' councils, and the educational policy of the town. If a community considers the teacher merely a person hired for cramming and giving grades, then it is the fault of the teaching profession itself. It has submitted too willingly to the American prejudice that the teacher should not mingle in public affairs, leaving the "pioneer spirit" to other citizens. For these and other reasons the task of the schools of education, especially those on the graduate level, will become greater and greater every year.

There has now emerged an increasing number of people I may call "efficiency experts," concerned with the improvement of teaching and teacher education. We should be grateful for their advice as far as it can help the schools of education and the public schools to achieve better results in the various subjects of the curriculum. But in their aversion to the discussion of the broader human goals of education these experts seem to forget that efficiency in learning, just as anywhere else, can be used for evil as well as for good purposes unless it helps the maturing person to understand the truth in Socrates' famous statement that the morally unexamined life is not worth living.

This continuing self-examination that should be required of every educated person will confront our teachers with problems that reach far beyond the immediate utility of this or that subject of learning. What, after all, is the purpose of learning? Merely to provide a "union card" for this or that vocation or profession, now generally called a "job," or also for the formation of a full and meaningful life? Sometimes it seems that the confessed atheist and the agnostic are more interested in these eternal problems of humanity than the conventional Christian and the satisfied and well-paid specialist.

If our departments of education fail to understand their

task of providing the competent and at the same time searching teacher, they will increase the dangers of modern mechanisation, conformism, and other depersonalizing trends in our modern civilization. If, on the other hand, they succeed in making the teacher conscious of his broad cultural mission, they will help our nation to survive both physically and spiritually and raise even the religious life of modern man to that stage of maturity where it is not at the present, despite millennia of history, but where, for mankind's sake, it should be.

NOTES

THE LEGAL ISSUE

1. Quoted in Anson Phelps Stokes, *Church and State in the United States* (New York: Harper, 1950), I, 529–530. For historical data I am indebted to this work and to Leo Pfeffer, *Church, State, and Freedom* (Boston: Beacon Press, 1953).

2. For the assessment bill, see Everson v. Board of Education, 330 U.S. 1, 72–74 (1947) (Appendix to opinion of Rutledge, J., quoting a copy of the bill preserved in the George Washington Papers, Library of Congress). For Jefferson's bill, see Stokes, *Church and State*, I, 333–334; H. J. Eckenrode, *Separation of Church and State in Virginia* (Richmond, Va., 1910), pp. 113–115.

3. Robert F. Drinan, *Religion, the Courts, and Public Policy* (New York: McGraw-Hill, 1963), p. 189.

4. *The Pilot*, June 7, 1952.

5. McCollum v. Board of Education, 333 U.S. 203, 227 (1948) (concurring).

6. State ex rel. Weiss v. School District of Edgerton, 76 Wis. 177, 199–200 (1890).

THE EDUCATIONAL ISSUE

1. *Milton on Education: The Tractate* of Education, *with Supplementary Extracts from Other Writings of Milton,* ed. Oliver Morley Ainsworth (Ithaca: Cornell University Press, 1928), pp. 55, 52.

2. William T. Marnell, *The First Amendment* (Garden City, N.Y.: Doubleday, 1964).

3. Franklin H. Littell, *From State Church to Pluralism* (Chicago: Aldine, 1962).

4. *Twelfth Annual Report of the Board of Education* [of the state of Massachusetts] *together with the Twelfth Annual Report of the Secretary of the Board* (Boston: Dutton and Wentworth, 1849), pp. 116–117. I am indebted for this quotation to Professor Jonathan C. Messerli of Teachers College, Columbia University.

For the best general treatment of this subject, see Raymond Culver, *Horace Mann and Religion in the Massachusetts Public Schools* (New Haven: Yale University Press, 1929).

5. Herman Wouk, *This Is My God* (Garden City, N.Y.: Doubleday, 1959).

6. See G. A. J. Rogers, "The Hypothesis of Harmony, An Interpretation of the Scientific Revolution in the Seventeenth Century," *The Listener,* February 18, 1965.

7. See in this context *Education and the Idea of Mankind,* ed. Robert Ulich (New York: Harcourt, Brace and World, 1964); and William Ernest Hocking, *The Coming World Civilization* (New York: Harper, 1956).

8. Robert Ulich, *On the Reform of Educational Research,* Harvard University, Graduate School of Education, Occasional Pamphlets (December 1937).

THE INGLIS LECTURES

1937   E. L. Thorndike. *The Teaching of Controversial Subjects.*

1939   C. A. Prosser. *Secondary Education and Life.*

1940   A. W. Williams. *Work, Wages, and Education.*

1945   G. F. Zook. *The Role of the Federal Government in Education.*

1946   Mark Starr. *Labor Looks at Education.*

1947   Ordway Tead. *Equalizing Educational Opportunities Beyond the Secondary School.*

1948   Allison Davis. *Social-Class Influences upon Learning.*

1949   Harold Benjamin. *The Cultivation of Idiosyncrasy.*

1950   Margaret Mead. *The School in American Culture.*

1951   Julius Seelye Bixler. *Education for Adversity.*

1952   Theodore M. Green. *Liberal Education Reconsidered.*

1953   Willard B. Spaulding. *The Superintendency of Public Schools—An Anxious Profession.*

1954   Henry Lee Smith. *Linguistic Science and the Teaching of English.*

1955   Henry Wyman Holmes. *". . . . the last best hope . . .": Democracy Makes New Demands on Education.*

1956   Vera Micheles Dean. *The American Student and the Non-Western World.*

1957   Horace Mann Bond. *The Search for Talent.*

1958   Max Beberman. *An Emerging Program of Secondary School Mathematics.*

THE BURTON LECTURES

1955   Hollis L. Caswell. *How Firm a Foundation? An Appraisal of Threats to the Quality of Elementary Education.*

1956   William S. Gray. *The Teaching of Reading: An International View.*

THE INGLIS AND BURTON LECTURES